Every
Entropy

Elena Rico Hernando

BookLeaf
Publishing

India | USA | UK

Presentation by *BookLeaf Publishing*

Web: www.bookleafpub.com

E-mail: info@bookleafpub.com

ISBN: 9789358313581

First edition 2023

DEDICATION

Let it be known, I fought my wars because you were by my side in the trenches.

ACKNOWLEDGEMENT

Had it not been for Pilu, Karen and Steve, I don't think I would have ever found a path in which I could explore my pain. For that I am immensely grateful. I owe my life and love to these greats.

I also know I need to thank Samuel for showing me how to see life in color and finding love in what surrounds me. Lastly, I would like to thank my mother and father, for fighting for me when I no longer wanted to fight. You will always hold the greatest space in my heart.

PREFACE

Coexisting with me is not an easy task. Let alone one I would want to endeavor in any way. The realities of mental illness mean that I feel everything to my core and yet I am unable to feel much at times. I hope that through these words, you can understand that I never chose to be the way I am. I never intended to lose so much, so young. I would give it all back in a moment.

From time to time, there are silver linings in my existence, even if they aren't evident. More so, I think anyone with deep routed trauma, grief and mental illness can tell you that these silver linings have been repressed through our own actions. I have let my thoughts bleed into these pages in hopes of finding something within me, anything at all. I guess you get to be the judge of whether or not I have succeeded. Choose wisely however, you never know in which shade of darkness you will see your finest reflection.

Within the lines

I wish I could paint by numbers
The areas of my brain
To christen the emotions that dance within my
soul
Have some perception of control
Paint within the lines
In the poem of color
Not a wild eruption to cover the canvas whole,
But gently position each brushstroke
Each hue in its chosen role
Oh how I wish
I could paint myself by numbers.

Monday

I have acute chronic major depressive disorder
Sometimes I smile and work away
I'll act like the darkness doesn't stay
And I'll be the perkiest on Mondays
And pretend that the boulder clay
Isn't
crushing my spine

Sometimes its hard to speak,
Cause the letters feel weak
As I string them along

Down the same path that Ive known
for far too long
Decades perhaps

But I'll be the first to pour you your morning
coffee
Oh but not me
I don't drink coffee
Coffee is a stimulant
That fact for you is innocent

For you coffee is coffee
For me coffee is cocaine
Cocaine is ten years ago
Ten years ago I still wasn't okay
But even coffee didn't numb the pain

So this decade I've taken on laughing
Like a sport
You play football, and I guess that works
But my spine has a dent
And I no longer drink coffee
So Ive taken up laughing

Until the cameras are turned off
When I no longer need to scoff
At what seems to be talk about the weather
Maybe they were talking about the weekend
Or work

Or that movie they loved
I wasn't really there

I mean I played the ball,
Smiled and agreed with it all
Only to then cry under bedsheets
The match was over
And I don't have any coffee to pour
Or a way to string the letters
Or a way to grow my wings' feathers
So my spine still aches all the same

But don't worry,
You said I looked happy on Sunday
So I'll be the perkiest me on Monday

A fire lit room in the dark

The freedom I feel when I am drifting
Only comes from time to time
Some say it's my calling
That I see a dark room in the light
Of a saturated sunrise

It's comes at a cost
To only see the curtains lifting
Feelings become brushstrokes and glowing eyes
That I don't often hide
The stitching in my heart becomes undone

The synapses in my brain never close
So I'll feel the warmth in your ice cold touch
The words you utter will make me blush
As my blood runs through my lungs
The smell of your naïve love will rush through
my pores

Forgive me if I don't see the iceberg
I'm simply blinded by the glimmer of the glitter
sea
I know it's not easy
To let one's skin unzip
To the sight of a dark room

I just don't see it the same
The dark looks like golden embers
Freedom, I call it

Even though it only comes from time to time
They say it's my calling.

Scottish winds

In the arms of Scottish winds,
My heart finds a new home,
A secret known only to our souls
The wind crisps my bone away
The rain washes away my skin
Drop by drop
Day by day

Somehow I find solace in the early sunsets
The hot chocolates you make,
The way we laugh under covers

Warm up each other
Yet many could not stand these winds

Not for the world's gold
Or skies of sapphire blue,
Would I trade the 3 o'clock dark,
My soggy socks
And you

Silent mases

Sometimes
All it takes
Is the silence
In the screaming crowd
To know
You only belong
In the cracks of your imagination
A social butterfly
Fluttering in
The masses of your
Empty palace

Collection of dust

You remain a book on my shelf
Collecting dust as the days pass by
The type of sentiment you keep
But you don't know why
I think I must have confused love and pain

In your pages
You show your true colors
How to be by your side
Was to drive down a braking bridge
Your hands no longer holding mine

Your wants for me
Never aligned with my needs
To be set free
From the cobwebs of your lies
Sometimes you fight
But I had to walk away
In order to survive

I no longer linger around
Trying to read your forbidden text
You washed my eyes
For too long
I can still distinguish your darkness
From my own

So I let the dust collect
To punish you
Even if you will never feel it
I got carpal tunnel from the pain
I'm glad you found what remains of your soul
But I won't be your witness

I will keep you on the shelf
Maybe one day I'll be strong enough
To take you down
Even if you are
The type of sentiment you keep
But I'll never understand why.

I didn't call

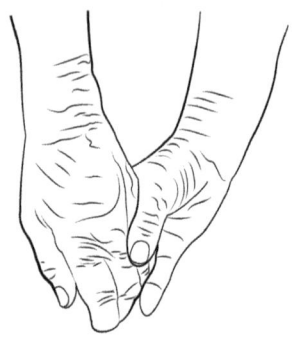

I am sorry I didn't call.
I let the dust collect around your vocal cords
I guess I didn't know how to tell you
That you led the path of light
In the pain they caused

I am sorry I didn't call,
Now you struggle to remember my name
Your eyes still glisten every time
I remind you
Of my love

I am sorry I didn't call,
I should've ask you
How to find peace
In the everlasting war
That is to be human

I am sorry I didn't call
I forgot that the embers of your mind
Would be blown away by time
And all I would have left
Is the string of words you are unable to say

I am sorry I didn't call,
To tell you I kept
The first, second and third
Drawing I made of you
When I was small

I am sorry I didn't call,
To engrave the sight of my warmth
In that brilliant mind of yours
I still feel the echos of your love
All these years later

When I now call,
You ask me the same thing
I find the light in your distant smile
Even if it is miles away
I braid your words into the loose strings of my
soul

It may seem meaningless now
But I'm sorry I didn't call.

Knuckles colliding

It's getting dark
I often tell myself I've lost the last
Embers of my spark
He always seems to know
When my eyes have clouded over

He stops my knuckles colliding
It can feel like he knows what I'm holding in
The demons I've been hiding
Before they wake me

He holds my aching breath
Exhales for me
In, two, three
Out, two, three

When the willows die
The cold air blows out my ashes
He wraps around my collection of dust
Lights a fire in the summer breeze
To warm me back together
Slowly I reform
To a lesser version of me I'm sure
But he's the kind of man
Who loves when I smile
Even if I'm crooked and broken in my mirror
He sees a different reflection

It's been over a year
When I feel the flame of my wet eyes
I look in the mirror
There are these marks next to my lips
The type that only can be seen
When you smile for what seems like
Forever

He still looks out for any ashes
To glue back to what I see as my clouded image
He tells me that I create the light
That reflects on my smile
So forevermore,
When it gets dark
He always stops my knuckles colliding.

Sometimes

Sometimes,
I wish things were different
Somedays,
I want all the minutes they stole
Spend them on a rainy day

Sometimes,
I look back in despair
To the little girl who thought it was okay
For your so called family
To love you that way

Sometimes

I wonder why I was so different
In a completely normal way
Because I want to be proud
Always be this loud

Sometimes
I wish I could let them go
The pain doesn't need to be there anymore
I am all grown now
Trying to catch up with their ghosts

Sometimes
I wish the pain made me value more
The family that I've grown
The ones who always stuck by me
The ones I've made my own

Sometimes,
It still hurts
But most times
I remember it's not my fault for leaving and
Loving the ones who are my home

Beauty in the Entropy

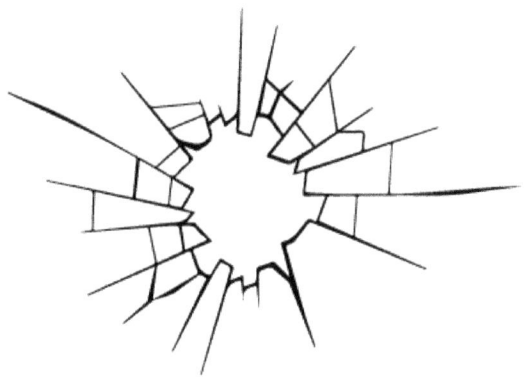

There is beauty
In the entropy of my grief.
I watch my past self shed from my skin,
I carry her mistakes
In one hand
In the other
The ashes she dusted off

So while I mourn her death
The jagged edges of your words
Will not break my skin

Like hers did
Despite the pain
This might cause
There is beauty in the entropy of my grief.

She did it for me

In the labyrinth of trials
An ember of her guides my steps.
She was drowning at sea
Amidst the crowd of her woes and
Insecurities

She was never taught to resow
The seams others had torn apart
So she let her hope pour from her edges
She tried to hold the weight of their wars
Neglecting the blood she had been bathed in

What remained a mystery to some
Was whilst she was coming undone
She wiped away her fears
All on her own
For seemingly no one
She longed to linger in obscurity
She ached for the solace of her own company

How did the fervor in her efforts persist,
even when she seemed unconcerned?
Behind every action,
A sonnet of intention must surely have been
composed
Why wage battles in the shadows
If not to unveil the stars' hidden stories?

I look back at her one last time,
The younger version of myself
Amidst uncertain storms
She braved the tempest's wrath
All for the sake of my tomorrow's path

She whispered her farewell to the fading night,
Certain of her own end
But sowed seeds of my dawn
Where her love
would forever ascend

So in my labyrinth of trials
Whenever my pulse quivers
Her sacrifice
A glowing ember within,
Lights my voyage through rebirth's endless sea
Toward the towering peak
Where dreams,
Untethered
Find their way to be

Greats

My voyage through life's tempestuous sea,
Nurtured and guided by the greats, I see,
In their towering wisdom, a radiant star,
I wouldn't have traversed this far
without who they are

Not the ones inked on parchment
Or bound in tomes,
These are stories untouched
By library domes
Unwritten legends
The world's hidden nooks,
These aren't the greats you read about in books

In their presence,
I learned that tears are a grace,
No need for the shadows of shame to embrace
They ignited a flame
A passionate decree
To guide my torn soul
To become the woman you see

My greats held my hand
On a Friday
When I could not stand
They unveiled the path to find my unique art,
In their wisdom,
I discovered my own part,

In their presence,
I found my genuine smile,
A world where the real me
Could stay for a while

My greats still stand by me
For them I would take the knee
To them I owe my life
For without these greats,
I'd fade away,
In their verses
I find my place to stay

Collision

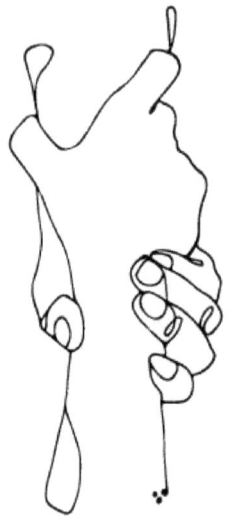

In two months it will be the third,
Three years ago is completely blurred
Back then talking about you was a constant buzz
in my head
Yet completely unheard
By the voices around me

Tears would fall to the sound of every Scottish
wind
Opening up seems like a sin
Now that the scarring is settling instead

I only think about you on every weekday
And the weekends
And the holidays

I've learned to carry you with me
Like rocks are carried by the sea
You only notice when they collide
The pain doesn't cease
But it subsides
Because collision can be beautiful

I think of you when birds fly by a broken nest
I think of you when I lie on my mothers chest
I think of you when someone complains about
an early morning
I think of you when I cry without any warning
I think I'll always think of you in some
dimension

I've learned that it doesn't have to hurt to
remember your smile
I've learned that grief can be versatile
So I'll think of you tonight, when the Scottish
winds blow
I'll cry by your memory tomorrow, when I feel
the world go slow
But my dear friend
I'll forever smile to the way you loved seeing
life's ill colored collisions

Perhaps

Nobody prepares you to be in that hospital bed,
You're eyes are tired of being puffy
And red
You break down often
Daily perhaps

Sometimes its hard to speak,
As I string words along
Down the same path that Ive known
for far too long
Decades perhaps

The road doesn't seem to cease
And all I'm asking for
Is peace
Peace of mind
A piece of yours perhaps

So when we say our piece,
We expect you to listen
To give us your time,
Not expect us to rhyme,
To shed light on this prison perhaps

We've fought our own wars
So when we muster up the courage,
Let our hearts pour
Listen without interruption,
A penny for our thoughts perhaps

Its taken me 16 years
To speak about these fears
To smile when I walk
To look at you when I talk
But perhaps

Perhaps,
Their eyes are still puffy,
Perhaps the keep looking for peace of mind and
can't find it

Perhaps they haven't figured out how to rhyme
Perhaps they won't look at you when their heart
pours
Maybe they cant ask you to not interrupt

And perhaps my path doesn't end until
You muster up the courage to ask
'A penny for your thoughts?'
Perhaps I understand the
Pain in their veins
More than you ever will
Perhaps

But I cant put a timeframe on recovery
I don't know at what point
 a hug will give them warmth
Again
But we'll listen,
We'll wait
To open the prison gate

So perhaps hug them tightly when they want it
Perhaps remember that it takes time to rhyme
Perhaps dry the puffiness away with tissues
Perhaps, let them speak or choose not to speak
Perhaps, show up to hold our hand
Or clap our successes
Because nobody prepares you to be in that
hospital bed

Tempest

I wonder,
If the feeling of crushing waves In the cavity of
my lungs,
Lasts forever
So in every fleeting breath of fresh air I take,
I convince myself
It is the last
Because that is simpler to understand
Than to acknowledge
One day,
The sea's tempestuous fury shall find
Its equal
In the gentle embrace of tranquil waters

Northern star

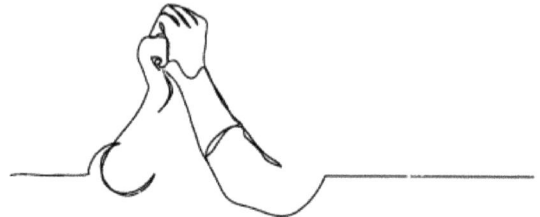

Did I miss the chance to find you?
To make you my guide, to show I care?
In a world of choices,
Did I overlook,
The constancy you offered,
The path you took?

Could I have looked up to you each night,
Found direction in what they describe
As your unwavering light?
When I was lost in the darkest of the fray,
Could your steady guidance have shown the
way?

Did I fail to make you my guiding star?
In life's chaos, did we drift too far?
I spent endless nights in the pews
I really wanted

To be your flesh too

I spend my days staring at the dark sky
Begging others for a reason why
Now, I wonder where you are,

Sorry

Im sorry

Sorry I couldn't make you my northern star.

Center ring

In life's grand circus,
I play a part,
A clown with a painted smile,
A heavy heart.
Behind the glass,
Where tears often flow,
I mime for laughter,
But they'll never know.
Beside the spotlight's glare,
I'm unseen.

I balance on wires,
Emotions on display,
The crowd applauds,
But I'm lost in the fray.

Beneath the makeup,
The jests, the jest,
I'm the clown who cries,
A soul distressed.
In the center ring,
My tears remain concealed.

No painted grin
Can hide my inner strife,
Invisible tears mark
The circus of life.

I yearn for a world
Where I can be free,
No more hiding behind the glass,
Just me.
For once,
 I wish to be truly seen.

Amidst the laughter
And the carnival's charms,
I'm a performer,
Caught in the world's arms.
Behind the façade,

My pain's kept in check,
As I dance through the shadows,
A somber silhouette.
Yet hope remains,
In the circus of my soul.

In this three-ring circus,
A solitary mime,
I bear a burden
In the midst of my prime.
Beneath the big top,
Where colors collide,
My silent sorrow
Is a sorrow I can't hide.
Yet I dream of a world
Where my tears can be shared.

Muse

Lead me to the shores
Where artists found their quiet end,
You and I
In harmony
Paint over our scars
A refuge to let sorrows fly
A sanctuary to release our cry
Just you and I
Lead me to the shores
Where artists found their quiet end.

Still here

Sometimes I vanish,
My corpse stays
Eyes wide open, responsive.
My body wants to remain lavish
For this, my person must enter a maze
One that allows all the
Deluded
Disgruntled
Dissociated
Versions of myself

I wish I could see that version of her
The grace and clarity it must take

To escape this monster, remain composed
While I'm just opaque
A hopeless author
That escapes
Expressionless
Enclosed
To all that surrounds me

I view her from the exterior
Screaming at the glass for her to let me in
Phantom tears roll down the idea that I am no
longer a person
Just a walking sin
My dissociated self is cheerier
Somewhat sardonic
Sophisticated
Sentient

Decades of enmity between my dissociation and
I.
I don't choose to vanish
It's a survival strategy

I wish I stayed

If you ever look at me and see her,
Wait it out
I'll be there somewhere

Give them a price

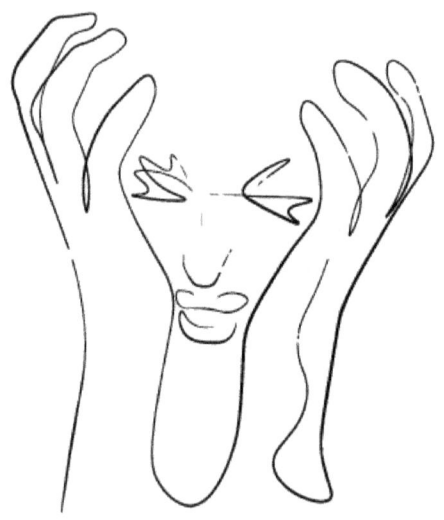

Put a price on my emotions
I'm trying to figure out
What I can buy
I suffocate in the motions
 Of my own drought
It hurts to try.

They tell me I'll be fine
 Its just a long haul
Flight to freedom
I'm starting to think

The sun might not shine
Happiness must not be my season.

I haven't much to spend
But I'd love to sip
A cup of Stable.

So anything you can lend
A lesson
or guidebook
On how not to trip over the same stone twice.

These stones remain ever present
I can pat off the dust
But I'd like to peal back
This fake smile
Borrow a real one for
A second of lust
Of the emotions I lack

So put a price on my emotions
 I might be able to trade
A lifetime of sorrow
For a real laugh
To water my drought.

When I ran away

I found the last text I sent you
Before I ran away
We didn't have much time
You saw the exit sign
I never meant to set
The world on fire

I remember when I saw you again
Only briefly
On that hospital bed
My hands felt damp
From my mother's tears
I couldn't respond

You looked at me
With the same tears in your eyes
That you had
The last day

But I found solace in your flame

I wanted to let you know
Wherever you are
That I'm still here
Maybe one day I'll come see you again
But I think I'll stay

Your hand still holds mine
I know you had to go
I hope you can understand
I couldn't leave them
Not yet

I wanted to let you know
Maybe
Just maybe
Someday,
I might find myself
Somehow
Somewhere
I might be fine